Published in the UK in 2014 by Focus Education (UK) Ltd

Focus Education (UK) Ltd
Talking Point Conference Centre
Huddersfield Road
Scouthead
Saddleworth
OL4 4AG

Focus Education (UK) Ltd  Reg. No 4507968

ISBN 978-1-909038-54-7

Companies, institutions and other organisations wishing to make bulk purchases of books published by Focus Education should contact their local bookstore or Focus Education direct:

Customer Services, Focus Education, Talking Point Conference & Exhibition Centre,
Huddersfield Road, Scouthead, Saddleworth, OL4 4AG
Tel 01457 821818  Fax 01457 878205

www.focus-education.co.uk
customerservice@focus-education.co.uk
Printed in Great Britain by Focus Education UK Ltd, Scouthead

# Focus Education (UK) Ltd: The Team

This new Learning Challenge Curriculum, taking account of the new National Curriculum (2014) has been created by the Focus Education team.

- Clive Davies, Director Focus Education
- Simon Camby, Chief Executive, Focus Academy Trust
- Keith Adams, Focus Education Consultant
- Paul Allen, Teacher, English Martyrs Catholic Primary, Derbyshire
- Jo Davies, Headteacher, Carr Mill Primary, St Helens
- Ros Ferrara, Focus Education Consultant
- Anne McNally, recently retired Headteacher, Wigan
- Tim Nelson, Focus Education Consultant
- Sarah Quinn, Focus Education Consultant
- Helen Rowland, Academy Improvement Officer, Focus Academy Trust

# Contents

# Introduction

- This book has been developed to support schools in applying the Learning Challenge principles to their teaching of Art and Design. It is based on the aims and subject content from the 2014 National Curriculum programmes of study for Key Stages One and Two.

- The questions outlined in the examples that follow are the starting points for you to consider. The ethos that underpins the Learning Challenge approach requires teachers to check on what children already know and then invite them to think of their own questions. Very importantly, ensure that all content absolutely meets your context.

- Each Learning Challenge has a suggested 'wow' and its own suggested reflection. By using these you will get a more complete level of challenge for the pupils.

- You will also note that every opportunity has been taken to suggest where children can apply knowledge, skills and understanding from other curriculum subjects where it is possible to do so.

- Finally, where a symbol   &#x1F4D6;   is seen, it will contain the name and author of a book recommended to be read when using the Learning Challenge.

# Learning Challenges – The Principles

*What are the main principles?*

- The Learning Challenge concept is built around the principle of greater learner involvement in their work. It requires deep thinking and encourages learners to work using a question as the starting point.

- In designing the curriculum teachers and learners are using a prime learning challenge, expressed as a question, as the starting point. Using the information gained from pre- learning tasks and the school's context a series of subsidiary challenges are then planned. Each subsidiary learning challenge is also expressed as a question. See how this works in the scheme of work provided.

- The subsidiary learning challenge is normally expected to last for one week but this does not need to be the case. However, initially it may be useful for the learners and indeed the staff to get used to the weekly learning challenge. The important point is that the learning challenges need to make sense to the learners and be something that is within their immediate understanding.

# Learning Challenges – The Principles

***How do the Pre- Learning Tasks Work?***

- Pre-Learning Tasks ensure that learners are directly involved in the planning process. Well planned pre-learning tasks should help to bring out what learners already know; what misconceptions they may have and what really interests them.

- Teachers should take account of the outcomes from pre-learning tasks to plan the subsidiary learning challenges for each major area of study. It should help teachers recognise what transferable skills learners have already developed that could be used to initiate new learning with a level of confidence.

- Pre-Learning tasks could take many different forms and can last for as long or as short as required. Some may be written tasks, others oral. Mind mapping is one method that has been used successfully by many schools. Using pre-learning tasks as part of a school's programme of home learning will help to get parents and carers directly involved in their children's learning.

# Learning Challenges – The Principles

*How are learners represented with opportunities to reflect on their learning?*

- Time for learners to reflect or review their learning is central to the whole process. This is in keeping with the 'Learning to Learn' principles where reflection is seen as a very important part of individuals' learning programme.

- Within the Learning Challenge Curriculum it is suggested that the final subsidiary learning challenge is handed over for learners to reflect on their learning. The idea is that learners represent their learning back to the rest of the class or another appropriate audience making the most of their oracy and ICT skills to do so. Initially, learners may require a great deal of direction so the reflection time may need to be represented in the form of a question which helps them to review their work.

- Although reflection is seen as a concluding part of the prime learning challenge, it is hoped that that there will be continual opportunities for learners to reflect frequently, especially as each subsidiary learning challenge comes to an end. Ideally, there should be a good deal of learner autonomy evident during reflection time.

The examples that follow are exactly that; they are examples.

There are six suggested Learning Challenges for each year group, so one could be taught per half-term if this suits the school's overall timetable.

For each year group there is one Learning Challenge per year based on each of the following themes: Drawing; Painting; Printing; Textiles; 3D; and Collage.

This has been designed to aid progression and also to ensure a balance of art and design themes over time. However, many of the requirements of the programme of study for each Key Stage will be relevant to each Learning Challenge and there is considerable overlap in skills and knowledge between the six headings used for the themes. Teachers should ensure that the children learn about the processes involved rather than concentrating only on the final product

Consider your context without losing sight of the National Curriculum
coverage when making adaptations to suit your school and the needs of your pupils.

# Art and Design: Key Stage One Overview

| Requirements from the Programme of Study |
|---|
| Pupils should be taught: |
| o to use a range of materials creatively to design and make products<br><br>o to use drawing, painting and sculpture to develop and share their ideas, experiences and imagination<br><br>o to develop a wide range of art and design techniques in using colour, pattern, texture, line, shape, form and space<br><br>o about the work of a range of artists, craft makers and designers, describing the differences and similarities between different practices and disciplines, and making links to their own work. |

# Art and Design: Key Stage One Overview

| | | Learning Challenges | | | | |
|---|---|---|---|---|---|---|
| | **Drawing** | **Painting** | **Printing** | **Textiles** | **3D** | **Collage** |
| **Year 1** | How do you feel in this picture? | How can we paint a firework display? | How can we print a meadow? | Where will our flying carpet take us? | What's that creepy crawly creature? | What will our underwater world look like? |
| **Year 2** | What is a 'still life' anyway? | How can we turn that photograph into a painting? | What will our wallpaper look like? | Where will we fly the class flag? | What will go inside and outside our pots? | What does *(the place we are learning about in geography)* look like? |

# Art and Design Learning Challenges

# Year 1

# Year 1: How do you feel in this picture?

**Drawing**
**To use drawing to develop and share their ideas, experiences and imagination.**

**WOW: Play games with the children where they have to guess how a person is feeling from the face they are making.**

| LC1 | Can we take photos of ourselves looking happy, sad, angry and any other feelings we can think of? |
| --- | --- |
| LC2 | Can we find drawings by famous artists showing peoples' feelings? |
| LC3 | What can we use to draw with and what effects can we produce? |
| LC4 | What materials will we use to produce our own drawings? |
| LC5 | What tips can we learn about drawing human faces? |
| LC6 | Can we practice drawing faces showing people's feelings and can we use software to draw faces as well? |
| LC7 | What do we need to remember as we draw our pictures? |
| Ref | Can we talk about what the people in our drawings are feeling? |

**Literacy Link:** Opportunities for the children to use books and websites to research.

**Mathematics Links:** Opportunities for the children to use language of measurement, fractions and Shape.

**Literacy Link:** Opportunities for the children to present orally or in writing.

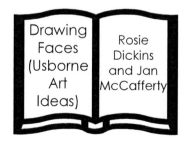

Drawing Faces (Usborne Art Ideas) Rosie Dickins and Jan McCafferty

Let's Make Faces Langeler, Grindell and Grindell

The Learning Challenge
**CURRICULUM**

# How do you feel in this picture?

## Year 1

### Drawing

- Can they communicate something about themselves in their drawing?
- Can they create moods in their drawings?
- Can they draw using pencil and crayons?
- Can they draw lines of different shapes and thickness, using 2 different grades of pencil?

### Use of IT

- Can they use a simple painting program to create a picture?
- Can they go back and change their picture?

### Knowledge

- Can they describe what they can see and like in the work of another artist?
- Can they ask sensible questions about a piece of art?

# Year 1: How can we paint a firework display?

**Painting**
**To use painting to develop and share their ideas, experiences and imagination.**

WOW: **Watch a film clip of a firework display.**

| | |
|---|---|
| LC1 | How can we use different paint brushes? |
| LC2 | Which colours can we see in pictures of fireworks and can we copy them using paint? |
| LC3 | How else can we apply paint to our firework pictures? |
| LC4 | Can we paint a large firework picture by working with our friends? |
| LC5 | Can we use software to create firework pictures? |
| LC6 | Which of our firework pictures do we think worked well and why? |
| Ref | Can we invite our parents or another class to our firework art gallery? |

**Mathematics Link:** Opportunities for the children to compare and order sizes of brushes and the marks they make.

**Oracy Link:** Opportunities for the children to discuss their work and justify their opinions.

**Literacy Links:** Opportunities for the children to write invitations and explain their artwork to an audience

Bonfire Night (Holidays and Festivals) — Nancy Dickmann

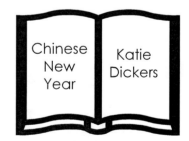

Chinese New Year — Katie Dickers

The Learning Challenge
**CURRICULUM**

# How can we paint a firework display?

## Year 1

### Painting

- Can they communicate something about themselves in their painting?
- Can they create moods in their paintings?
- Can they choose to use thick and thin brushes as appropriate?
- Can they paint a picture of something they can see?
- Can they name the primary and secondary colours?

### Use of IT

- Can they use a simple painting program to create a picture?
- Can they use tools like fill and brushes in a painting package?
- Can they go back and change their picture?

### Knowledge

- Can they ask sensible questions about a piece of art?

# Year 1: How can we print a meadow?

<u>Printing</u>
**To develop a wide range of art and design techniques in using colour, pattern, texture, line, shape, form and space.**

WOW: **Visit a flower shop, garden centre or flower meadow and draw different flowers.**

| | |
|---|---|
| LC1 | Can we draw the shapes of different flowers and petals? |
| LC2 | What colours do we need for our prints? |
| LC3 | What shapes do we need for our printing blocks? |
| LC4 | Can we print a meadow on paper or card? |
| LC5 | How can we print a set of greetings cards? |
| LC6 | Can we print on textiles to make flower-patterned curtains? |
| Ref | How can we use our printing skills to make a cover for our art work folders? |

**Science Link:** This Learning Challenge could be taught together with the 'What birds and animals would Little Red Riding Hood find in our park?' Science Learning Challenge.

**Geography Link:** Opportunities for the children to learn about flowers that grow in different Places.

**Mathematics Links:** Opportunities for the children to use the language of shape and comparative Sizes.

First Arts And Crafts: Printing   Sue Stocks

The Learning Challenge
**CURRICULUM**

# How can we print a meadow?

## Year 1

### Printing

- Can they print with sponges, vegetables and fruit?
- Can they print onto paper and textile?
- Can they design their own printing block?
- Can they create a repeating pattern?

### Use of IT

- Can they use a simple painting program to create a picture?
- Can they use tools like fill and brushes in a painting package?
- Can they go back and change their picture?

### Knowledge

- Can they describe what they can see and like in the work of another artist?
- Can they ask sensible questions about a piece of art?

# Year 1: Where will our flying carpet take us?

**Textiles**
**Pupils should be taught:**
**To use a range of materials creatively to design and make products.**

WOW: **Read a story involving magical journeys or transportation.**

| | |
|---|---|
| LC1 | Do we know any stories that have a flying carpet in the plot? |
| LC2 | What patterns, colours and designs are used in carpets and rugs? |
| LC3 | Can we draw a design for our own mini flying carpet? |
| LC4 | What is weaving and can we practice our design by weaving paper strips? |
| LC5 | Can we chose colours and fabrics to use to weave our own mini flying carpets? |
| LC6 | How will we decorate the edges of our flying carpets? |
| Ref | Can we draw our flying carpet and ourselves having an adventure? |

**Literacy Link:** Opportunities for the children to re-tell stories.

**Mathematics Links:** Opportunities for the children to measure, compare sizes and discuss the properties of patterns and shapes.

**Literacy Link:** Opportunities for the children to tell and write their own stories.

Arts And Crafts: Weaving — Susie O'Reilly

The Learning Challenge
**CURRICULUM**

# Where will our flying carpet take us?

## Year 1

### Textiles

- Can they sort threads and fabrics?
- Can they group fabrics and threads by colour and texture?
- Can they weave with fabric and thread?

### Drawing

- Can they communicate something about themselves in their drawing?
- Can they draw using pencil and crayons?
- Can they draw lines of different shapes and thickness, using 2 different grades of pencil?

# Year 1: What's that creepy crawly creature?

**3D**
**Pupils should be taught:**
**To use a range of materials creatively to design and make products.**

WOW: **Go on a mini-beast hunt around the school grounds.**

| | |
|---|---|
| LC1 | What creepy, crawly creatures live around our school and can I draw them? |
| LC2 | What tools and techniques will help us make our models of the creatures out of modelling clay? |
| LC3 | How can we make different shapes as well as rough and smooth textures? |
| LC4 | Can we make our models in the colours of our creatures? |
| LC5 | How will we make sure our model looks just like the real creature? |
| LC6 | Can we design and make a background to display our finished models? |
| Ref | Can we explain how we made our models? |

**Science Links:** Links with living things and habitats.

**Mathematics Link:** Opportunities for the children to compare the features of different creatures numerically.

**Literacy Links:** Opportunities for the children to develop their vocabulary as they describe features.

**Literacy Link:** Opportunities for the children to present to an audience.

Playing With Plasticine — Barbara Reid

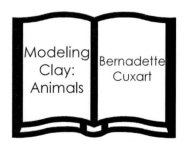

Modeling Clay: Animals — Bernadette Cuxart

## The Learning Challenge
# CURRICULUM

# What's that creepy crawly creature?

## Year 1

### 3D

- Can they add texture by using tools?
- Can they make different kinds of shapes?
- Can they cut, roll and coil materials such as clay, dough or plasticine?

### Use of IT

- Can they use a simple painting program to create a picture?
- Can they use tools like fill and brushes in a painting package?
- Can they go back and change their picture?

### Knowledge

- Can they describe what they can see and like in the work of another artist?
- Can they ask sensible questions about a piece of art?

# Year 1: What will our underwater world look like?

**Collage**
**Pupils should be taught:**
**To develop a wide range of art and design techniques in using colour, pattern, texture, line, shape, form and space.**

WOW: **Visit an aquarium or pet fish shop or go pond dipping.**

| | |
|---|---|
| LC1 | What lives under the sea or in a pond and can we draw them? |
| LC2 | What colours and textures can we see? |
| LC3 | Can we use software to make an underwater picture? |
| LC4 | What materials could we use to make a collage of an underwater world? |
| LC5 | How will we cut and stick our materials? |
| LC6 | Can we work together to produce a large collage? |
| Ref | What parts of our collage do we like best and why? |

**Science Link:** Opportunities for the children to learn about habitats.

**Literacy Link:** Opportunities for the children to develop vocabulary and spelling of adjectives.

**Oracy Link:** Opportunities for the children to talk to an audience and justify their ideas and opinions

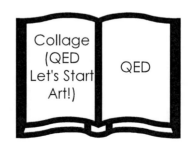

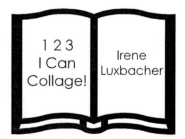

The Learning Challenge
**CURRICULUM**

# What will our underwater world look like?

## Year 1

### Collage

- Can they cut and tear paper and card for their collages?
- Can they gather and sort the materials they will need?

### Use of IT

- Can they use a simple painting program to create a picture?
- Can they use tools like fill and brushes in a painting package?
- Can they go back and change their picture?

### Knowledge

- Can they describe what they can see and like in the work of another artist?
- Can they ask sensible questions about a piece of art?

# Art and Design Learning Challenges

# Year 2

# Year 2: What is a 'still life' anyway?

**Drawing**
**To use drawing to develop and share their ideas, experiences and imagination.**

WOW: **Show a slideshow of still life drawings from a range of artists.**

| | |
|---|---|
| LC1 | Which artists are famous for their still life work? |
| LC2 | What objects would we choose to draw and what materials shall we use? |
| LC3 | How do you use a viewfinder? |
| LC4 | How can we make the objects we draw look light or dark or shiny or rough? |
| LC5 | Can we sketch our drawings first? |
| LC6 | What techniques will we use for our final drawing? |
| Ref | How will we display our finished drawings? |

**Literacy Link:** Opportunities for the children to use books and websites to research.

**History Link:** Opportunities for the children to learn about the historical context of the artist and their work.

**Computing Link:** The children could display their drawings on the school website

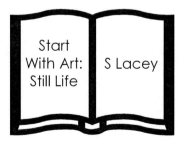

Start With Art: Still Life    S Lacey

The Learning Challenge
**CURRICULUM**

# What is a 'still life' anyway?

## Year 2

### Drawing

- Can they use three different grades of pencil in their drawing (4B, 8B, HB)?
- Can they use charcoal, pencil and pastels?
- Can they create different tones using light and dark?
- Can they show patterns and texture in their drawings?
- Can they use a viewfinder to focus on a specific part of an artefact before drawing it?

### Use of IT

- Can they create a picture independently?
- Can they use simple IT mark-making tools, e.g. brush and pen tools?
- Can they edit their own work?
- Can they take different photographs of themselves displaying different moods?
- Can they change their photographic images on a computer?

### Knowledge

- Can they link colours to natural and man-made objects?
- Can they say how other artists have used colour, pattern and shape?
- Can they create a piece of work in response to another artist's work?

# Year 2: How can we turn that photograph into a painting?

**Painting**

**To use painting to develop and share their ideas, experiences and imagination.**

**WOW: Take photos of the class and use software to alter the pictures and then make them appear to be painted.**

| | |
|---|---|
| LC1 | What makes a good photograph and what will we choose as a subject? |
| LC2 | Can we use software to improve our photographs? |
| LC3 | Can we sketch our photographs? |
| LC4 | What colours can we see in our photographs and can we make some of them by mixing paints? |
| LC5 | What is the effect of adding black or white to different colours? |
| LC6 | Which painting techniques will we use to complete our pictures? |
| Ref | Do our pictures closely match our photographs? |

**Geography or History Link:** Opportunities for the children to take photos linked to their work in these subjects.

**Mathematics Links:** Opportunities for the children to measure quantities of paints.

Fun with Art: Learn How to Draw and Paint — Helen Webster

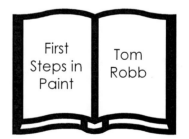

First Steps in Paint — Tom Robb

The Learning Challenge
**CURRICULUM**

# How can we turn that photograph into a painting?

## Year 2

### Painting

- Can they mix paint to create all the secondary colours?
- Can they mix and match colours and predict outcomes?
- Can they mix their own brown?
- Can they make tints by adding white?
- Can they make tones by adding black?

### Use of IT

- Can they create a picture independently?
- Can they use simple IT mark-making tools, e.g. brush and pen tools?
- Can they edit their own work?
- Can they take different photographs of themselves displaying different moods?
- Can they change their photographic images on a computer?

### Knowledge

- Can they link colours to natural and man-made objects?
- Can they say how other artists have used colour, pattern and shape?
- Can they create a piece of work in response to another artist's work?

# Year 2: What will our wallpaper look like?

**Printing**
To develop a wide range of art and design techniques in using colour, pattern, texture, line, shape, form and space.

WOW: **Watch a film clip of a commercial printing press at work.**

| | |
|---|---|
| LC1 | What wallpaper patterns and designs do we like? |
| LC2 | Can we design our own wallpaper patterns by drawing and by using software? |
| LC3 | What printing techniques can we learn? |
| LC4 | Which wallpaper design will we choose to print and what technique will we use? |
| LC5 | Can we print with more than one colour in our design? |
| LC6 | Can we produce two sections of patterned wallpaper that will fit together neatly? |
| Ref | How does our wallpaper look hanging on a wall? |

**Oracy Link:** Opportunities for the children to discuss and then justify their choices.

**Mathematics Links:** Opportunities for the children to measure and use the properties of 2D shapes.

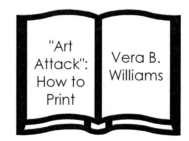

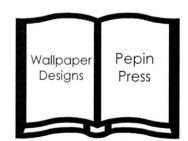

The Learning Challenge
**CURRICULUM**

# What will our wallpaper look like?

## Year 1

### Printing

- Can they create a print using pressing, rolling, rubbing and stamping?
- Can they create a print like a designer?

### Use of IT

- Can they create a picture independently?
- Can they use simple IT mark-making tools, e.g. brush and pen tools?
- Can they edit their own work?

### Knowledge

- Can they link colours to natural and man-made objects?
- Can they say how other artists have used colour, pattern and shape?
- Can they create a piece of work in response to another artist's work?

# Year 2: Where will we fly the class flag?

**Textiles**
**Pupils should be taught:**
**To use a range of materials creatively to design and make products.**

WOW: **Watch official and religious ceremonies that involve flags.**

| | |
|---|---|
| LC1 | Why do we have flags? |
| LC2 | Can we draw and colour some flags from around the world and from sports clubs and other organisations? |
| LC3 | Can we design a flag for ourselves? |
| LC4 | How will we make our own flag by sewing and gluing? |
| LC5 | What design will we use for a class flag? |
| LC6 | Which part of our class flag will we each make and how will we join it all together? |
| Ref | Where will our flag fly and what does it mean? |

**History Link:** Opportunities for the children to learn about the significance of flags in history.

**Geography Link:** Opportunities for the children to investigate flags from different countries.

**Computing Link:** Opportunities for the children to use software to design their flags.

Flags (Usborne Spotter's Guide) William Crampton

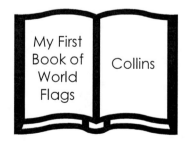
My First Book of World Flags Collins

The Learning Challenge
**CURRICULUM**

# Where will we fly the class flag?

## Year 2

**Textiles**

- Can they join fabric using glue?
- Can they sew fabrics together?
- Can they create part of a class patchwork?

**Use of IT**

- Can they create a picture independently?
- Can they use simple IT mark-making tools, e.g. brush and pen tools?
- Can they edit their own work?

**Knowledge**

- Can they link colours to natural and man-made objects?
- Can they say how other artists have used colour, pattern and shape?

# Year 2: What will go inside and outside our pots?

**3D**
**Pupils should be taught:**
**To use a range of materials creatively to design and make products.**

WOW: **Visit a museum to see ceramics or view online.**

| | |
|---|---|
| LC1 | How have clay pots changed or not changed over time? |
| LC2 | How are clay pots decorated and can we copy some designs? |
| LC3 | What will our clay pots look like? |
| LC4 | What tools and techniques will help us make our finger pots? |
| LC5 | How can we decorate our pots using tools to add line and texture and using paint to add colour? |
| LC6 | Are there other ways to make clay pots? |
| Ref | How do our pots compare with pots made by other artists? |

**Literacy and Computing Link:** Opportunities for the children to use books and websites to research.

**History Links:** Opportunities for the children to learn about pottery used in a period in history or locally in the past.

**Geography and History Links:** Opportunities for the children to investigate pottery design from different places and periods in time.

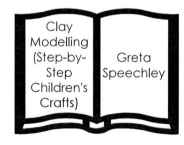

Clay Modelling (Step-by-Step Children's Crafts) Greta Speechley

Clay (Let's Create!) Anna Llimos Plomer

The Learning Challenge
**CURRICULUM**

# What will go inside and outside our pots?

## Year 2

### 3D

- Can they make a clay pot?
- Can they join two finger pots together?
- Can they add line and shape to their work?

### Knowledge

- Can they link colours to natural and man-made objects?
- Can they say how other artists have used colour, pattern and shape?
- Can they create a piece of work in response to another artist's work?

# Year 2: What does *(the place we are learning about in geography)* look like?

**Collage**
**Pupils should be taught:**
**To develop a wide range of art and design techniques in using colour, pattern, texture, line, shape, form and space.**

WOW: **Watch a slideshow of amazing pictures from places around the world.**

| | |
|---|---|
| LC1 | What can we see in *(the place we are learning about in geography)*? |
| LC2 | Can we draw and colour a view of the place and use software to produce a picture too? |
| LC3 | What patterns and textures can we see there? |
| LC4 | What materials could we use to make a collage of a view? |
| LC5 | Can we make individual collages? |
| LC6 | How can we all contribute to a class collage? |
| Ref | Can we identify features of *(the place we a learning about in geography)* in our collage? |

**Geography Links:** Links with the study of a locality or region.

**Literacy Links:** Opportunities for the children to develop their vocabulary and write descriptions.

**Oracy Link:** Opportunities for the children to discuss and share opinions.

Making Collage (Action Art) — Isabel Thomas

Collage (Step-by-Step Children's Crafts) — Judy Balchin

The Learning Challenge
**CURRICULUM**

# What does (*the place we are learning about in geography*) look like?

## Year 2

### Collage

- Can they create individual and group collages?
- Can they use different kinds of materials on their collage and explain why they have chosen them?
- Can they use repeated patterns in their collage?

### Use of IT

- Can they create a picture independently?
- Can they use simple IT mark-making tools, e.g. brush and pen tools?
- Can they edit their own work?
- Can they change their photographic images on a computer?

### Knowledge

- Can they link colours to natural and man-made objects?

# Art and Design: Key Stage Two Overview

## Requirements from the Programme of Study

Pupils should be taught:

o to develop their techniques, including their control and their use of materials, with creativity, experimentation and an increasing awareness of different kinds of art, craft and design

o to create sketch books to record their observations and use them to review and revisit ideas

o to improve their mastery of art and design techniques, including drawing, painting and sculpture with a range of materials (for example, pencil, charcoal, paint, clay)

o about great artists, architects and designers in history.

# Art: Key Stage Two Overview

| | Drawing | Painting | Printing | Textiles | 3D | Collage |
|---|---|---|---|---|---|---|
| **Learning Challenges** | | | | | | |
| **Year 3** | Could we be book illustrators? | What's that coming over the hill? | How can we string together a printed picture? | How cosy is our quilt? | What is in front of the mask? | How can collage help us make a book for younger children? |
| **Year 4** | How can we bring our drawings to life? | Which famous artists lived near here? | Would people send our greetings cards? | How can we change the colour of that fabric? | How will we make our museum exhibits? | How will our mosaics improve the look of our school? |
| **Year 5** | Where's the detail in that picture? | How did the great artists see themselves? | How will we screen print our own posters? | What will our wall hanging celebrate? | Has thou slain the Jabberwock? | What will make our rainforest stand out? |
| **Year 6** | How can we design our own font? | Can you spray that again please? | What will we print on our leavers' t-shirts? | What can we recycle to make a recycling banner? | Could we create a model Minecraft school? | What did buildings look like back then? |

The Learning Challenge™
CURRICULUM

# Art and Design Learning Challenges

# Year 3

# Year 3: Could we be book illustrators?

**Drawing**
**Pupils should be taught:**
**To improve their mastery of art and design techniques, including drawing,**

WOW: **Use a high quality picture book to discuss the story and convey the importance of illustration to the children.**

| | |
|---|---|
| LC1 | Why are illustrations in books important? |
| LC2 | Who are the famous book illustrators? |
| LC3 | Can we copy the style of two or three different illustrators that we like? |
| LC4 | What are the important things to remember when we draw an illustration and what part of a story shall we illustrate? |
| LC5 | How can sketches help us develop our final illustration? |
| LC6 | Can we use technology to copy our finished illustrations and insert them into a page of text? |
| Ref | What does an audience think of our illustrations? |

**Literacy and Computing Link:** Opportunities for the children to use books and websites to research.

**Literacy Link:** Opportunities for the children to examine the text carefully and ensure their illustration matches the meaning.

**Literacy Links:** Opportunities for the children to illustrate their own stories for an audience.

Step-by-Step Drawing Book / Fiona Watt And Candice Whatmore

Quentin Blake (Tell Me About) / Chris Powling

The Learning Challenge
**CURRICULUM**

# Could we be book illustrators?

## Year 3

### Drawing

- Can they show facial expressions in their drawings?
- Can they use their sketches to produce a final piece of work?
- Can they write an explanation of their sketch in notes?
- Can they use different grades of pencil shade, to show different tones and texture?

### Sketch books

- Can they use their sketch books to express feelings about a subject and to describe likes and dislikes?
- Can they make notes in their sketch books about techniques used by artists?
- Can they suggest improvements to their work by keeping notes in their sketch books?

### Use of IT

- Can they use the printed images they take with a digital camera and combine them with other media to produce art work?
- Can they use IT programs to create a piece of work that includes their own work and that of others (using web)?
- Can they use the web to research an artist or style of art?

### Knowledge

- Can they compare the work of different artists?
- Can they explore work from other cultures?
- Can they explore work from other periods of time?
- Are they beginning to understand the viewpoints of others by looking at images of people and understand how they are feeling and what the artist is trying to express in their work?

# Year 3: What's that coming over the hill?

**Painting**
**Pupils should be taught:**
To develop their techniques, including their control and their use of materials, with creativity, experimentation and an increasing awareness of different kinds of art, craft and design.

WOW: **Use viewing frames for the children to select views they particularly like around the school or on a trip or visit.**

| | |
|---|---|
| LC1 | What is a landscape picture? |
| LC2 | Who are some of the famous landscape painters? |
| LC3 | How have landscapes been painted in other times and places? |
| LC4 | What is perspective? |
| LC5 | Which particular styles of landscape painting do we like? |
| LC6 | Can we sketch our own landscape pictures and mix paints to colour them? |
| LC7 | How can digital photography help us paint landscape pictures? |
| LC8 | Can we produce two contrasting landscape paintings? |
| Ref | Can we produce a guide to landscape painting? |

**Geography and History Links:** Opportunities for the children to find out about landscape art from a place or region they are studying.

**Oracy Links:** Opportunities for the children to discuss and justify their choices.

**Literacy Link:** Opportunities for the children to develop writing for an audience.

The Learning Challenge
**CURRICULUM**

## Year 3

### Painting

- Can they predict with accuracy the colours that they mix?
- Do they know where each of the primary and secondary colours sits on the colour wheel?
- Can they create a background using a wash?
- Can they use a range of brushes to create different effects?

### Sketch books

- Can they make notes in their sketch books about techniques used by artists?
- Can they suggest improvements to their work by keeping notes in their sketch books?

### Use of IT

- Can they use the printed images they take with a digital camera and combine them with other media to produce art work?
- Can they use IT programs to create a piece of work that includes their own work and that of others (using web)?
- Can they use the web to research an artist or style of art?

### Knowledge

- Can they compare the work of different artists?
- Can they explore work from other cultures?
- Can they explore work from other periods of time?
- Are they beginning to understand the viewpoints of others by looking at images of people and understand how they are feeling and what the artist is trying to express in their work?

# Year 3: How can we string together a printed picture?

**Printing**
**Pupils should be taught:**
**To improve their mastery of art and design techniques.**

**WOW:** **Demonstrate string printing on a large scale using rope or thick cord.**

| | |
|---|---|
| LC1 | How can we print with string? |
| LC2 | What effect do different types of string have on our prints? |
| LC3 | What pictures could we print and what can't we print using this technique? |
| LC4 | How can we print using more than one colour? |
| LC5 | Can we repeat the same print accurately? |
| LC6 | How will we display our finished prints? |
| Ref | What are the positive and negatives of string printing as a technique? |

**Literacy Links:** Opportunities for the children to design and print pictures for book covers using this technique.

**Computing Link:** Opportunities for the children to use software to explore and design using repeating patterns.

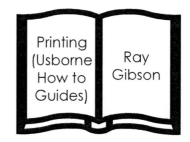

Printing (Usborne How to Guides)   Ray Gibson

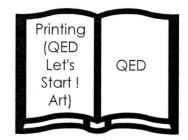

Printing (QED Let's Start ! Art)   QED

The Learning Challenge
**CURRICULUM**

## How can we string together a printed picture?

### Year 3

**Printing**

- Can they make a printing block?
- Can they make a 2 colour print?

# Year 3: How cosy is our quilt?

**Textiles**
**Pupils should be taught:**
To improve their mastery of art and design techniques, including drawing, painting and sculpture with a range of materials.

WOW: **Visit a bed shop or interior furnishing shop and ask the children to record the patterns and designs they see.**

| | |
|---|---|
| LC1 | What can we find out about quilts and how they are designed and made? |
| LC2 | Can we copy and develop some patterns we have found in quilts? |
| LC3 | How can we develop patterns and designs using software? |
| LC4 | Why are there different types of stitching and how many can we learn to use? |
| LC5 | Which fabrics could we use and what effect do they have? |
| LC6 | What patterns could we use for our own class quilt? |
| LC7 | How can we cut and join each section of the quilt? |
| Ref | How does our quilt compare with ones you can buy? |

**Literacy Link:** Opportunities for the children to use books and websites to research.

**Mathematics Links:** Opportunities for the children to measure lengths and compare angles.

**Literacy Link:** Opportunities for the children to write a report or summary.

The Learning Challenge
**CURRICULUM**

# How cosy is our quilt?

## Year 3

### Textiles

- Can they use more than one type of stitch?
- Can they join fabric together to form a quilt using padding?
- Can they use sewing to add detail to a piece of work?

### Sketch books

- Can they use their sketch books to express feelings about a subject and to describe likes and dislikes?
- Can they make notes in their sketch books about techniques used by artists?
- Can they suggest improvements to their work by keeping notes in their sketch books?

### Use of IT

- Can they use the printed images they take with a digital camera and combine them with other media to produce art work?
- Can they use IT programs to create a piece of work that includes their own work and that of others (using web)?

# Year 3: What is in front of the mask?

**3D**
**Pupils should be taught:**
To develop their techniques, including their control and their use of materials, with creativity, experimentation and an increasing awareness of different kinds of art, craft and design.

WOW: **Show a variety of masks and discuss their design and purpose.**

| | |
|---|---|
| LC1 | How are masks used in different cultures and places? |
| LC2 | Can we copy some designs for masks? |
| LC3 | What will our own masks look like? |
| LC4 | What materials will we use to create our masks? |
| LC5 | How will we decorate our masks? |
| LC6 | Can we use software to create simple masks based on photographs? |
| Ref | Can we use our masks in a performance or show? |

**Geography and History Links:** Opportunities for the children to learn about the use of masks in a historical period or in a particular region or country.

**Literacy and Dance Links:** Opportunities for the children to write scripts, perform for an audience and evaluate their performances.

Making Masks (Kids Can Do It) Renee Schwarz

Make Your Own Art: Making Masks Sally Henry and Trevor Cook

The Learning Challenge
**CURRICULUM**

# What is in front of the mask?

## Year 3

### 3D

- Can they add onto their work to create texture and shape?
- Can they work with life size materials?

### Sketch books

- Can they make notes in their sketch books about techniques used by artists?
- Can they suggest improvements to their work by keeping notes in their sketch books?

### Use of IT

- Can they use the printed images they take with a digital camera and combine them with other media to produce art work?
- Can they use IT programs to create a piece of work that includes their own work and that of others (using web)?

### Knowledge

- Can they explore work from other cultures?
- Can they explore work from other periods of time?
- Are they beginning to understand the viewpoints of others by looking at images of people and understand how they are feeling and what the artist is trying to express in their work?

# Year 3: How can collage help us make a book for younger children?

**Collage**
**Pupils should be taught:**
**To improve their mastery of art and design techniques, including drawing, painting and sculpture with a range of materials.**

WOW: **Show the children the illustrations from 'The Very Hungry Caterpillar'.**

| | |
|---|---|
| LC1 | How does Eric Carle use collage to make his illustrations? |
| LC2 | Which other artists use collage and what can we learn from them? |
| LC3 | Can we sketch ideas for our own story book layout for younger children? |
| LC4 | What materials will we use to develop our own style of collage? |
| LC5 | Can we work together to create our own story books using collage? |
| Ref | Did the younger children enjoy our books? |

**Literacy Links:** Opportunities for the children to use books and websites to research.

**Literacy Link:** Opportunities for the children to Interview younger children and report their findings.

Let's Do Art: Having Fun With Collage — Sarah Medina

The Learning Challenge
**CURRICULUM**

# How can collage help us make a book for younger children?

## Year 3

### Collage

- Can they cut very accurately?
- Can they overlap materials?
- Can they experiment using different colours?
- Can they use mosaic?
- Can they use montage?

### Sketch books

- Can they use their sketch books to express feelings about a subject and to describe likes and dislikes?
- Can they make notes in their sketch books about techniques used by artists?
- Can they suggest improvements to their work by keeping notes in their sketch books?

### Knowledge

- Can they compare the work of different artists?

# Art and Design Learning Challenges

# Year 4

# Year 4: How can we bring our drawings to life?

**Drawing**
**Pupils should be taught:**
**To improve their mastery of art and design techniques, including drawing.**

WOW: **Show the children an artist's or art student's sketch pad.**

| | |
|---|---|
| LC1 | What do we know about different drawing materials and their effects? |
| LC2 | Can we draw an object using shading to show texture? |
| LC3 | How can we show shadow and reflection in our sketches and drawings? |
| LC4 | Can we apply our drawing skills when we draw pictures of people? |
| LC5 | How do artists show movement in their art work and what can we learn from this? |
| LC6 | How can we draw pictures of people in action and give the viewer the impression of movement? |
| Ref | What are our 'Top Tips' for drawing brilliant pictures? |

**Oracy Link:** Opportunities for the children to discuss, justify and give explanations.

**Science Link:** Opportunities for the children to learn about the properties of light.

**Literacy Link:** Opportunities for the children to write a guide to developing drawing skills.

Art Smart: Draw it! Wendy Walker

Make Your Mark: The Drawing Book for Children Sarah Richardson

The Learning Challenge
**CURRICULUM**

# How can we bring our drawings to life?

## Year 4

### Drawing

- Can they begin to show facial expressions and body language in their sketches?
- Can they identify and draw simple objects, and use marks and lines to produce texture?
- Can they organise line, tone, shape and colour to represent figures and forms in movement?
- Can they show reflections?
- Can they explain why they have chosen specific materials to draw with?

### Sketch books

- Can they use their sketch books to express their feelings about various subjects and outline likes and dislikes?
- Can they produce a montage all about themselves?
- Do they use their sketch books to adapt and improve their original ideas?
- Do they keep notes about the purpose of their work in their sketch books?

### Knowledge

- Can they experiment with different styles which artists have used?
- Can they explain art from other periods of history?

# Year 4: Which famous artists lived near here?

**Painting**
**Pupils should be taught:**
**About great artists, architects and designers in history.**

WOW: **Visit a local art gallery.**

**History Link:** This Learning Challenge could be taught alongside a local history Learning Challenge.

| | |
|---|---|
| LC1 | Which famous artists lived in our town/city/county/region? |
| LC2 | What can we find out about their life and their influences? |
| LC3 | Can we sketch in the style of a famous local artist? |
| LC4 | What painting techniques did a famous local artist use? |
| LC5 | How can we produce our own paintings in the style of a famous local artist? |
| Ref | Can we produce a timeline of their lives with our own versions of their paintings as well as copies of the originals? |

**Literacy Links:** Opportunities for the children to use books and websites to research.

**History Link:** Opportunities for the children to refer to other events that were happening both nationally and internationally at points in the timeline.

The Learning Challenge
**CURRICULUM**

# Which famous artists lived near here?

## Year 4

### Painting

- Can they create all the colours they need?
- Can they create mood in their paintings?
- Do they successfully use shading to create mood and feeling?

### Sketch books

- Can they use their sketch books to express their feelings about various subjects and outline likes and dislikes?
- Can they produce a montage all about themselves?
- Do they use their sketch books to adapt and improve their original ideas?
- Do they keep notes about the purpose of their work in their sketch books?

### Knowledge

- Can they experiment with different styles which artists have used?
- Can they explain art from other periods of history?

# Year 4: Would people send our greetings cards?

**Printing**
**Pupils should be taught:**
**To improve their mastery of art and design techniques.**

WOW: **Show the children a range of greetings cards and discuss their designs and purpose.**

| | |
|---|---|
| LC1 | Which greeting card designs do we like and why? |
| LC2 | What drawing skills will we use and what is the effect of colour? |
| LC3 | Can we sketch some designs for our own cards? |
| LC4 | Which designs will we print and what printing technique should we use? |
| LC5 | Can we use four or more colours in our prints and still print accurately? |
| LC6 | Can we repeat our card design successfully? |
| LC7 | Can we design a logo for our own greetings card 'company' and print it onto bags, posters and other materials? |
| Ref | How will we advertise our hand crafted greeting cards? |

**Literacy Links:** Opportunities for the children to discuss their ideas and justify their opinions.

**Literacy and Music Links:** Opportunities for the children to write adverts and jingles for an advert.

Printing - Step-by-Step Children's Craft Series — Michelle Powell

Art and Craft Skills: Printing — Hachette Children's Books

The Learning Challenge
**CURRICULUM**

# Would people send our greetings cards?

## Year 4

### Printing

- Can they print using at least four colours?
- Can they create an accurate print design?
- Can they print onto different materials?

### Sketch books

- Can they use their sketch books to express their feelings about various subjects and outline likes and dislikes?
- Do they use their sketch books to adapt and improve their original ideas?
- Do they keep notes about the purpose of their work in their sketch books?

### Knowledge

- Can they experiment with different styles which artists have used?

# Year 4: How can we change the colour of that fabric?

**Textiles**
**Pupils should be taught:**
To improve their mastery of art and design techniques, including drawing, painting and sculpture with a range of materials.

WOW: **Staff wear tie-dyed t-shirts and other very bright clothing.**

| | |
|---|---|
| LC1 | What fabric dying techniques can we find out about? |
| LC2 | What are batik and tie-dying and can we use these techniques? |
| LC3 | What will we make from our dyed fabrics? |
| LC4 | How will we cut and join the fabric once it is dyed? |
| LC5 | How will we display our final products? |
| Ref | Can we explain how to dye fabrics to an audience? |

**Literacy Link:** Opportunities for the children to use books and websites to research.

**History and Geography Links:** Opportunities for the children to learn about fabric dying in other places and cultures and also in other periods in history.

**Literacy Links:** Opportunities for the children to speak to their peers or younger children or to write their own 'How to dye fabric' guide booklet.

Start to Batik / Rosi Robinson

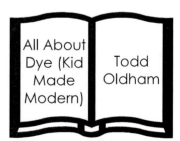

All About Dye (Kid Made Modern) / Todd Oldham

The Learning Challenge
**CURRICULUM**

# How can we change the colour of that fabric?

## Year 4

**Textiles**

- Can they use early textile and sewing skills as part of a project?

**Knowledge**

- Can they experiment with different styles which artists have used?
- Can they explain art from other periods of history?

# Year 4: How will we make our museum exhibits? *

## *This unit links with whichever historical period the children are studying.

**3D**
**Pupils should be taught:**
To develop their techniques, including their control and their use of materials, with creativity, experimentation and an increasing awareness of different kinds of art, craft and design.

WOW: **Visit a museum or take a virtual tour of a museum.**

| | |
|---|---|
| LC1 | What artefacts and artwork did *the people we are studying* produce and what materials, tools and techniques did they use? |
| LC2 | Can we draw examples of artefacts or artwork in our sketch books to show specific features and to show the same item from different viewpoints? |
| LC3 | Which artefacts will we make replicas of and what materials and techniques will we use? |
| LC4 | Can we combine different materials to help us make our 3D replicas? |
| LC5 | What painting and finishing techniques will be most effective? |
| Ref | How will we open our museum to other members of our school? |

**Literacy Link:** Opportunities for the children to use books and websites to research.

**Mathematics Links:** Opportunities for the children to put artefacts and artwork in the context of a timeline and calculate time intervals between events.

**Literacy Links:** Opportunities for the children to write invitations, guidebooks and information labels for their class museum.

Eyewitness Guides — Dorling Kindersley

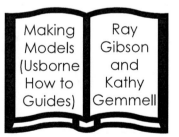

Making Models (Usborne How to Guides) — Ray Gibson and Kathy Gemmell

The Learning Challenge
**CURRICULUM**

# How will we make our museum exhibits?

## Year 4

### 3D

- Do they experiment with and combine materials and processes to design and make 3D form?
- Can they begin to sculpt clay and other mouldable materials?

### Sketch books

- Do they use their sketch books to adapt and improve their original ideas?
- Do they keep notes about the purpose of their work in their sketch books?

### Knowledge

- Can they experiment with different styles which artists have used?
- Can they explain art from other periods of history?

# Year 4: How will our mosaics improve the look of our school?

**Collage**
**Pupils should be taught:**
**To improve their mastery of art and design techniques, including drawing, painting and sculpture with a range of materials.**

WOW: **Show the children examples of ceramic mosaic work.**

| | |
|---|---|
| LC1 | Can we find examples of ceramic mosaics that inspire us? |
| LC2 | Where will our own ceramic mosaics be located and what will be the theme? |
| LC3 | Can we sketch ideas for our own mosaics? |
| LC4 | Is there software that can help us develop our own ideas and designs? |
| LC5 | Which colours and textures will we use and why are they effective? |
| LC6 | What techniques will we use to make our mosaic? |
| Ref | What are people's reactions to our finished mosaics? |

**History Link:** This could be taught alongside the 'Why were the Romans so powerful and what did we learn from them?' Learning Challenge

**Computing Link:** Opportunities for the children to use websites to research.

**Mathematics Links:** Opportunities for the children to measure areas of the school to calculate the overall dimensions of their mosaics.

**Literacy Link:** Opportunities for the children to write questionnaires or plan questions prior to interviewing people.

Mosaics (Step-by-step Children's Crafts) Michelle Powell

Amazing Mosaics S. Kelly

The Learning Challenge
**CURRICULUM**

# How will our mosaics improve the look of our school?

## Year 4

### Collage

- Can they use ceramic mosaic to produce a piece of art?
- Can they combine visual and tactile qualities?

### Sketch books

- Do they use their sketch books to adapt and improve their original ideas?
- Do they keep notes about the purpose of their work in their sketch books?

### Use of IT

- Can they create a piece of art work which includes the integration of digital images they have taken?
- Can they combine graphics and text based on their research?

### Knowledge

Can they experiment with different styles which artists have used?
Can they explain art from other periods of history?

# Art and Design Learning Challenges

# Year 5

# Year 5: Where's the detail in that picture?

**Drawing**
**Pupils should be taught:**
**To improve their mastery of art and design techniques, including drawing.**

WOW: **Show the children detailed pencil drawings such as 'Praying Hands' by Durer, or google 'pencil drawings' for examples by a range of artists.**

| | |
|---|---|
| LC1 | What materials should every good artist have in their art set for drawing? |
| LC2 | Can we complete the other half of a black and white photograph using pencil drawing and shading techniques? |
| LC3 | Can we sketch the same object from three different viewpoints, using line and shading to show texture and detail? |
| LC4 | How could we improve our sketches? |
| LC5 | Which sketch will we choose to develop into a finished picture? |
| Ref | How will we display our drawings to best effect and to a wider audience? |

**Literacy Link:** The children could write instructions for drawing, including the materials needed and their purpose.

**Mathematics Links:** Opportunities for the children to investigate angles and measurement.

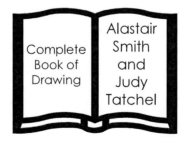

The Learning Challenge
**CURRICULUM**

# Where's the detail in that picture?

## Year 5

### Drawing

- Can they identify and draw simple objects, and use marks and lines to produce texture?
- Do they successfully use shading to create mood and feeling?
- Can they organise line, tone, shape and colour to represent figures and forms?
- Can they show reflections?
- Can they explain why they have chosen specific materials to draw with?

### Sketch books

- Do they keep notes in their sketch books as to how they might develop their work further?
- Do they use their sketch books to compare and discuss ideas with others?

### Knowledge

- Can they experiment with different styles which artists have used?
- Do they learn about the work of others by looking at their work in books, the Internet, visits to galleries and other sources of information?

# Year 5: How did the great artists see themselves?

**Painting**
**Pupils should be taught:**
**To develop their techniques, including their control and their use of materials, with creativity, experimentation and an increasing awareness of different kinds of art, craft and design.**

WOW: **Show the children a range of self-portraits by famous artists and see if they can match the artist to information about that artist, the time they lived and their associated style.**

| | |
|---|---|
| LC1 | What can we find out about a great artist and their self-portraits? |
| LC2 | Can we copy a self-portrait in the style of a great artist? |
| LC3 | Can we each make a photo montage to show our personalities? |
| LC4 | How can our photos help us develop sketches for our own self-portrait? |
| LC5 | Would mood or emotion do we want to portray and what techniques will help us achieve this? |
| LC6 | Which colours will we need to make for our palette ? |
| LC7 | What painting techniques will we use? |
| Ref | Can we discuss each others' self-portraits and the emotions we are portraying? |

**Literacy Link:** Opportunities for the children to use books and websites to research.

**Computing Link:** Opportunities for the children to use software to manipulate and publish their work.

The Learning Challenge
**CURRICULUM**

# How did the great artists see themselves?

## Year 5

### Drawing

- Can they create all the colours they need?
- Can they create mood in their paintings?
- Can they express their emotions accurately through their painting and sketches?

### Sketch books

- Do they keep notes in their sketch books as to how they might develop their work further?
- Do they use their sketch books to compare and discuss ideas with others?

### Knowledge

- Can they experiment with different styles which artists have used?
- Do they learn about the work of others by looking at their work in books, the Internet, visits to galleries and other sources of information?

# Year 5: How will we screen print our own posters?

**Printing**
**Pupils should be taught:**
To improve their mastery of art and design techniques, including drawing, painting and sculpture with a range of materials.

WOW: **Show a slideshow of classic advertising posters in a range of styles.**

| | |
|---|---|
| LC1 | Which poster designs and designers are famous and why? |
| LC2 | How did poster design change through the 19$^{th}$ and 20$^{th}$ centuries? |
| LC3 | Can we design a range of posters for a class or school event, using our sketch books? |
| LC4 | Which posters will we choose to print and why? |
| LC5 | What is screen printing? |
| LC6 | How will we screen print our posters? |
| Ref | How do our posters compare with the classic designs poster designs? |

**Literacy Links:** Opportunities for the children to use books and websites to research.

**History Link:** Opportunities for the children to learn about local businesses and how they advertised in the past.

**Literacy Link:** Opportunities for the children to compare, contrast and report their findings.

The Learning Challenge
**CURRICULUM**

# How will we screen print our own posters?

## Year 5

### Printing

- Can they print using a number of colours?
- Can they create an accurate print design that meets a given criteria?

### Sketch books

- Do they keep notes in their sketch books as to how they might develop their work further?
- Do they use their sketch books to compare and discuss ideas with others?

### Knowledge

- Can they experiment with different styles which artists have used?
- Do they learn about the work of others by looking at their work in books, the Internet, visits to galleries and other sources of information?

# Year 5: What will our wall hanging celebrate?

**Textiles**
**Pupils should be taught:**
**To improve their mastery of art and design techniques, including drawing, painting and sculpture with a range of materials.**

WOW: **Visit an art gallery or historic site with tapestries or wall hangings, or go on a virtual tour of an art gallery, exhibition or historic site.**

| | |
|---|---|
| LC1 | What event will our wall hanging celebrate? |
| LC2 | Can we sketch some possible designs? |
| LC3 | How can IT help us capture and develop our ideas for the wall hanging? |
| LC4 | What sewing skills do we already have and what do we need to learn? |
| LC5 | What fabrics will we use and what other materials could we use as decoration? |
| LC6 | How will we ensure we all contribute to the final wall hanging? |
| Ref | Can we organise an unveiling of our finished work? |

**History Link:** This could link with the anniversary of a historic event at a local or national level.

**Mathematics Links:** Opportunities for the children to use measurements in context to ensure all parts of the final wall hanging fit together and are of the correct scale.

**Literacy Link:** Opportunities for the children to write letters and invitations.

Sewing For Kids: Easy Projects to Sew at Home — Alice Butcher and Ginny Farquhar

Stories In Art: Tapestries and Textiles — Louise Spilsbury and Rob Childs

The Learning Challenge
**CURRICULUM**

# What will our wall hanging celebrate?

## Year 5

### Textiles

- Can they use textile and sewing skills as part of a project, e.g. hanging, textile book, etc.? This could include running stitch, cross stitch, backstitch, appliqué and/or embroidery.

### Sketch books

- Do they keep notes in their sketch books as to how they might develop their work further?
- Do they use their sketch books to compare and discuss ideas with others?

### Use of IT

- Can they create a piece of art work which includes the integration of digital images they have taken?
- Can they scan images and take digital photos, and use software to alter them, adapt them and create work with meaning.

### Knowledge

- Can they experiment with different styles which artists have used?
- Do they learn about the work of others by looking at their work in books, the Internet, visits to galleries and other sources of information?

# Year 5: Has thou slain the Jabberwock?

**3D**
**Pupils should be taught:**
**To improve their mastery of art and design techniques, including drawing, painting and sculpture with a range of materials (for example, pencil, charcoal, paint, clay)**

WOW: **Arrange for the children to view and handle a range of model fantasy figures and models made from a range of media.**

| | |
|---|---|
| LC1 | What might the creatures in the poem 'Jabberwocky' look like and can we sketch our ideas? |
| LC2 | Which material would be best for making our figures and why? |
| LC3 | What tools and techniques will help us make our 3D models? |
| LC4 | Can we make models of two or three of the creatures from the poem using a different material for each model? |
| LC5 | What type of paint and painting techniques will we use for our finished models? |
| LC6 | Can we make a display for our models with a quote from the poem? |
| Ref | Can we animate our models and make a short film of a verse from the poem? |

**Literacy Links:** Links with the study of a classic poem.

**Science Link:** Opportunities for the children to discuss the properties of different materials.

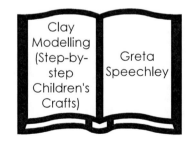

Clay Modelling (Step-by-step Children's Crafts) — Greta Speechley

You Can Draw Fantasy Figures: Drawing Dungeon Creatures — Steve Sims

The Learning Challenge
**CURRICULUM**

# Has thou slain the Jabberwock?

## Year 5

### 3D

- Do they experiment with and combine materials and processes to design and make 3D form?
- Can they sculpt clay and other mouldable materials?

### Sketch books

- Do they keep notes in their sketch books as to how they might develop their work further?
- Do they use their sketch books to compare and discuss ideas with others?

### Use of IT

- Can they create digital images with animation, video and sound to communicate their ideas?

### Knowledge

- Do they learn about the work of others by looking at their work in books, the Internet, visits to galleries and other sources of information?

# Year 5: What will make our rainforest stand out?

**Collage**
**Pupils should be taught:**
**To improve their mastery of art and design techniques, including drawing, painting and sculpture with a range of materials.**

WOW: **Share a range of high quality photographs of rainforests with the children.**

| | |
|---|---|
| LC1 | How can software help us manipulate a photograph of the rainforest to improve the picture? |
| LC2 | Can we sketch leaves, plants and rainforest animals? |
| LC3 | Which famous artists have used collage as a technique? |
| LC4 | Which picture will we develop into a collage? |
| LC5 | What materials will we choose and why? |
| LC6 | How will we work as a team to develop our collages? |
| LC7 | Can we also make a small ceramic collage with a rainforest theme? |
| Ref | What advice would we give people who want to make collages? |

**Geography Links:** Links with Learning Challenge 'Why should the rainforest be important to us all?'

**Computing Link:** Opportunities for the children to publish their pictures online.

**Literacy Link:** Opportunities for the children to research and write biographies.

**Literacy Link:** Opportunities for the children to write instructions, guides or information leaflets.

Art Attack: How to Collage

Karen Brown

The Learning Challenge
**CURRICULUM**

# What will make our rainforest stand out?

## Year 5

### Collage

- Can they use ceramic mosaic to produce a piece of art?
- Can they combine visual and tactile qualities?

### Sketch books

- Do they keep notes in their sketch books as to how they might develop their work further?
- Do they use their sketch books to compare and discuss ideas with others?

### Use of IT

- Can they create a piece of art work which includes the integration of digital images they have taken?
- Can they combine graphics and text based on their research?
- Can they scan images and take digital photos, and use software to alter them, adapt them and create work with meaning.

### Knowledge

- Can they experiment with different styles which artists have used?
- Do they learn about the work of others by looking at their work in books, the Internet, visits to galleries and other sources of information?

The Learning Challenge™
CURRICULUM

# Art and Design Learning Challenges

# Year 6

# Year 6: How can we design our own font?

**Drawing**
**Pupils should be taught:**
**To improve their mastery of art and design techniques, including drawing.**

**WOW: Look at examples of illuminated manuscripts and discuss the techniques and materials used.**

| | |
|---|---|
| LC1 | Why are there so many fonts available and what effect do they have on the audience? |
| LC2 | Can we sketch designs for fonts for three different audiences? |
| LC3 | What could we include in an illuminated font design that reflects our personalities and achievements in Primary School? |
| LC4 | What drawing techniques can we use as we develop our designs? |
| LC5 | Can we draw designs for each letter of our name in our chosen 'illuminated manuscript' font? |
| LC6 | How can we use software to develop our font designs? |
| Ref | Can we explain why our font reflects our personality and experiences? |

**Literacy Link:** Opportunities for the children to discuss their ideas and research from books and websites

**Oracy Link:** Opportunities for the children to present to an audience.

How To Draw Anything    Mark Linley

Let's Write!: Design Your Own Fonts    Julia Kaergel

The Learning Challenge
**CURRICULUM**

## Year 6

### Drawing

- Do their sketches communicate emotions and a sense of self with accuracy and imagination?
- Can they explain why they have combined different tools to create their drawings?
- Can they explain why they have chosen specific drawing techniques?

### Sketch books

- Do their sketch books contain detailed notes, and quotes explaining about items?
- Do they compare their methods to those of others and keep notes in their sketch books?
- Do they combine graphics and text based research of commercial design, for example, magazines to influence the layout of their sketch books?
- Do they adapt and refine their work to reflect its meaning and purpose, keeping notes and annotations in their sketch books?

### Use of IT

- Do they use software packages to create pieces of digital art to design.
- Can they create a piece of art which can be used as part of a wider presentation?

### Knowledge

- Can they make a record about the styles and qualities in their work?
- Can they say what their work is influenced by?

# Year 6: Can you spray that again please?

**Painting**
**Pupils should be taught:**
to develop their techniques, including their control and their use of materials, with creativity, experimentation and an increasing awareness of different kinds of art, craft and design.

WOW: **Have a class debate about whether it is always right or wrong for people to paint graffiti on buildings etc.**

| | |
|---|---|
| LC1 | What can we find out about the history of graffiti and famous graffiti artists? |
| LC2 | Can we record aspects of graffiti art we particularly like in our sketch books? |
| LC3 | Can we design and paint our own tag? |
| LC4 | Which piece of graffiti art will we copy using paints? |
| LC5 | Is it possible to use software to produce the effects of graffiti artwork? |
| LC6 | Can we paint our own version of a classical picture in the style of a contemporary graffiti artist? |
| Ref | What laws would we change or make about graffiti if we were in charge? |

**Computing Link:** Opportunities for the children to use books and websites to research.

**History Link:** Opportunities for the children to place both pieces of art within their historical contexts.

**Literacy Links:** Opportunities for the children to debate and justify their opinions.

Radar: Art on the Street: Graffiti Culture — Liz Gogerly

Real-life Stories: Banksy — Hettie Bingham

The Learning Challenge
**CURRICULUM**

# Can you spray that again please?

## Year 6

### Painting

- Can they explain what their own style is?
- Can they use a wide range of techniques in their work?
- Can they explain why they have chosen specific painting techniques?

### Sketch books

- Do their sketch books contain detailed notes, and quotes explaining about items?
- Do they compare their methods to those of others and keep notes in their sketch books?
- Do they combine graphics and text based research of commercial design, for example, magazines to influence the layout of their sketch books?
- Do they adapt and refine their work to reflect its meaning and purpose, keeping notes and annotations in their sketch books?

### Use of IT

- Do they use software packages to create pieces of digital art to design.
- Can they create a piece of art which can be used as part of a wider presentation?

### Knowledge

- Can they make a record about the styles and qualities in their work?
- Can they say what their work is influenced by?
- Can they include technical aspects in their work, e.g. architectural design?

# Year 6: What will we print on our leavers' t-shirts?

**Printing**
**Pupils should be taught:**
**To improve their mastery of art and design techniques.**

WOW: **Staff wear vibrant printed clothing in different styles and in contrast to their normal clothes.**

| | |
|---|---|
| LC1 | Which printed t-shirt designs do we like and why? |
| LC2 | Can we sketch some designs for what we could print on our own leavers' t-shirts? |
| LC3 | Which software can help us develop our designs? |
| LC4 | What will our finished design look like? |
| LC5 | What techniques will we use to print onto textiles, using more than one colour? |
| LC6 | How effective has our printing process been and what have we learnt? |
| Ref | Can we organise a fashion show to model our finished t-shirts? |

**Mathematics Links:** Opportunities for the children to compare the costs of different clothes and the costs of having t-shirts printed commercially.

**Literacy Link:** Opportunities for the children to write invitations and reviews.

All About Fabric Printing — Todd Oldham

The Ultimate T-shirt Book — Deborah Morgenthal

The Learning Challenge
**CURRICULUM**

# What will we print on our leavers' t-shirts?

## Year 6

### Printing

- Can they overprint using different colours?
- Do they look very carefully at the methods they use and make decisions about the effectiveness of their printing methods?

### Sketch books

- Do their sketch books contain detailed notes, and quotes explaining about items?
- Do they compare their methods to those of others and keep notes in their sketch books?
- Do they combine graphics and text based research of commercial design, for example magazines, to influence the layout of their sketch books?
- Do they adapt and refine their work to reflect its meaning and purpose, keeping notes and annotations in their sketch books?

### Use of IT

- Do they use software packages to create pieces of digital art to design.

### Knowledge

- Can they make a record about the styles and qualities in their work?
- Can they say what their work is influenced by?

# Year 6: What can we recycle to make a recycling banner?

**Textiles**
**Pupils should be taught:**
**To improve their mastery of art and design techniques, including drawing, painting and sculpture with a range of materials.**

WOW: **Visit a textile recycling centre.**

| | |
|---|---|
| LC1 | What designs can we sketch for a banner that celebrates and promotes recycling? |
| LC2 | Can we use software to help us develop our ideas? |
| LC3 | Which design will we choose and why? |
| LC4 | How will we encourage people to give us fabric and textiles they no longer need? |
| LC5 | How will we include the widest range of textiles in our banner as possible? |
| LC6 | How will we use colour and contrast in our banner? |
| LC7 | What techniques will we use to join our textiles to make our banner? |
| Ref | What are people's reactions to our banner? |

**Computing Links:** Opportunities for the children to use websites to research and software to enhance and manipulate their designs.

**Literacy Link:** Opportunities for the children to write letters and persuade an audience.

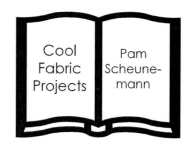

Cool Fabric Projects

Pam Scheune-mann

The Learning Challenge
**CURRICULUM**

# What can we recycle to make a recycling banner?

## Year 6

### Textiles

- Can they include both visual and tactile elements in their work?

### Sketch books

- Do their sketch books contain detailed notes, and quotes explaining about items?
- Do they compare their methods to those of others and keep notes in their sketch books?
- Do they combine graphics and text based research of commercial design, for example magazines, to influence the layout of their sketch books?
- Do they adapt and refine their work to reflect its meaning and purpose, keeping notes and annotations in their sketch books?

### Use of IT

- Do they use software packages to create pieces of digital art to design.

### Knowledge

- Can they make a record about the styles and qualities in their work?
- Can they say what their work is influenced by?

# Year 6: Could we create a model Minecraft school?

**3D**
**Pupils should be taught:**
**To develop their techniques, including their control and their use of materials, with creativity, experimentation and an increasing awareness of different kinds of art, craft and design.**

WOW: **Use Minecraft and ask the children to help the teacher design a classroom.**

| | |
|---|---|
| LC1 | What is special about the design of Minecraft? |
| LC2 | Can we sketch what parts of our school would look like in Minecraft? |
| LC3 | Can we develop a sketch into a drawing and finished coloured picture? |
| LC4 | How could we use modelling materials to make 3D models and colour them to look like Minecraft 'products'? |
| LC5 | Can we construct a model of part of our school to look like a Minecraft screenshot in 3D? |
| LC6 | Can we publish pictures of our models online? |
| Ref | If we designed our own online world, what would it look like? |

**Science Link:** Opportunities for the children to discuss the properties of different materials.

The Ultimate Player's Guide to Minecraft — Stephen O'Brien

The 3-D Paper Book — Hannah Tofts

The Learning Challenge
**CURRICULUM**

# Could we create a model Minecraft school?

## Year 6

### 3D

- Can they create models on a range of scales?
- Can they create work which is open to interpretation by the audience?

### Sketch books

- Do their sketch books contain detailed notes, and quotes explaining about items?
- Do they compare their methods to those of others and keep notes in their sketch books?
- Do they combine graphics and text based research of commercial design, for example magazines, to influence the layout of their sketch books?
- Do they adapt and refine their work to reflect its meaning and purpose, keeping notes and annotations in their sketch books?

### Use of IT

- Do they use software packages to create pieces of digital art to design.
- Can they create a piece of art which can be used as part of a wider presentation?

### Knowledge

- Can they make a record about the styles and qualities in their work?
- Can they say what their work is influenced by?
- Can they include technical aspects in their work, e.g. architectural design?

# Year 6: What did buildings look like back then?*

### *This unit links with whichever historical period the children are studying.

<u>Collage</u>
**Pupils should be taught:**
**To improve their mastery of art and design techniques, including drawing, painting and sculpture with a range of materials.**

WOW: **Look at architects drawings and blueprints of buildings.**

| | |
|---|---|
| LC1 | Can we sketch buildings from *the historical period we are studying*? |
| LC2 | What building materials were used and how can we show texture in our drawings? |
| LC3 | Which software can help us draw 3D designs of buildings? |
| LC4 | How can we use perspective to make our collages appear 3D? |
| LC5 | Which materials will we use for a collage of the buildings? |
| LC6 | How will we attach the materials to make our collage? |
| Ref | Do our collages accurately represent buildings from *the historical period we are studying*? |

**History Links:** Links with the historical periods the children are studying and may include the study of local history.

**Literacy Link:** Opportunities for the children to use books and websites to research.

**Science Links:** Opportunities for the children to discuss the properties of different materials.

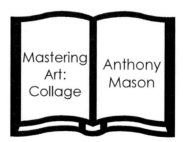
Mastering Art: Collage — Anthony Mason

The Learning Challenge
**CURRICULUM**

## Year 6

### Collage

- Can they justify the materials they have chosen?
- Can they combine pattern, tone and shape?

### Sketch books

- Do their sketch books contain detailed notes, and quotes explaining about items?
- Do they compare their methods to those of others and keep notes in their sketch books?
- Do they combine graphics and text based research of commercial design, for example magazines etc, to influence the layout of their sketch books?
- Do they adapt and refine their work to reflect its meaning and purpose, keeping notes and annotations in their sketch books?

### Use of IT

- Do they use software packages to create pieces of digital art to design.
- Can they create a piece of art which can be used as part of a wider presentation?

### Knowledge

- Can they make a record about the styles and qualities in their work?
- Can they say what their work is influenced by?
- Can they include technical aspects in their work, e.g. architectural design?